To....Dad.....................

LOVE
From.....Helen, Sam t

Cam open
xxx

GW00706066

Purple Ronnie's
Reasons Why You're a
SUPER DAD

LOVE YOU

by Purple Ronnie

First published 2010 by Boxtree
an imprint of Pan Macmillan, a division of Macmillan Publishers Limited
Pan Macmillan, 20 New Wharf Road, London N1 9RR
Basingstoke and Oxford
Associated companies throughout the world
www.panmacmillan.com

ISBN 978-0-7522-2721-4

9 8 7 6 5 4 3 2 1

A CIP catalogue record for this book is
available from the British Library.

Printed and bound in Hong Kong

'Purple Ronnie' created by Giles Andreae. The right of Giles Andreae and Janet Cronin
to be identified respectively as the author and illustrator of this work has been asserted by them
in accordance with the Copyright, Designs and Patents Act 1988.

Visit **www.panmacmillan.com** to read more about all our books
and to buy them. You will also find features, author interviews and
news of any author events, and you can sign up for e-newsletters
so that you're always first to hear about our new releases.

a poem for a

Top Dad

Here's a little message
For a dad who is the tops
It's to tell you that you're
smashing
And to say I love you lots!

a poem for my
D a d

Being a dad is a difficult job
That's not always easy to do
But if I could choose the
　　best dad in the world
I'm sure I would go and pick
　　　　you!

Reading on the
toilet is a dad thing.
Tough luck if he's
into long books

a poem for my
D.I.Y. Dad

When light bulbs fail
and fuses blow

Don't stress- it's not that
bad

'Cos look who's coming
with his toolkit...
Yes! It's Handy Dad!

a poem to say you've

Still Got It

You may be getting wrinkly,
Dad
And have a chubby tum
But you're not past it yet
because...
I caught you cuddling Mum!

Some dads like to share their hobbies with the whole family

a poem for my

Great Dad

You're a five star taxi service

You're a handy cash point too

So here's a massive thank you

To a dad as great as you

a poem about my dad's

Car Love

My Dad drives a sad old heap

Which rattles, whines and
squeaks

But in his dreams his
sports car gleams

As in it, off he streaks...!

PARALLEL UNIVERSE

Some dads try to be trendy. This can be embarrassing

a poem about

My Fab Dad

Why don't you put your feet up
And take the day off too
Cos it must be very hard
to be

A dad as fab as YOU!

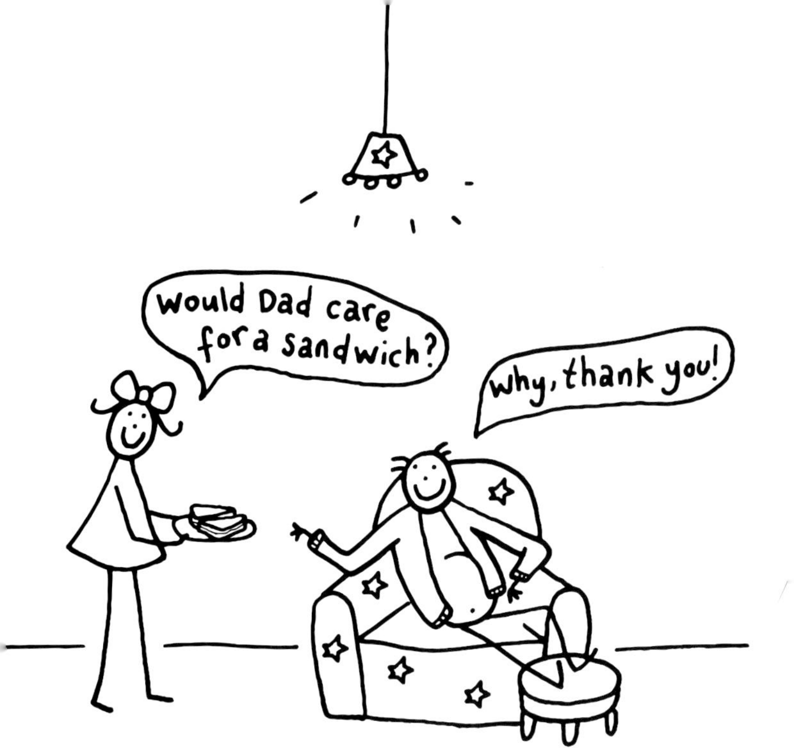
would Dad care for a sandwich?
why, thank you!

a poem about

Dad at Home

Dad says he works his socks off

Is that why they're so smelly?

And is that why, when he's back home,
He's always watching telly?

Your dad may offer you
driving lessons for free.
This does not always work.

a poem about

Dad's Stuff

Most dads have a special
drawer
Crammed full of useful bits.
Whenever something breaks
at home
Dad's got the part that
fits

a poem about

Dad's Cooking

When Dad decides to make
a meal

He's like a Master Cook

He makes a top class curry
BUT...

...the mess he makes - just look!

Teenage daughters don't always realise that their friends can make their Dad feel quite nervous and shy

a poem about

Dad Love

Dads can be embarrassing

And Dads can be a bore

But you're a really fab one

And I couldn't love you more!

the best →

a poem for

My Dad

You're supercool, good-looking
As clever as can be
And guess what dad - the
best thing is
You've passed it all to me!

Dad often thinks HIS
music is the best

a poem for my

Wonderful Dad

I know that it sounds cheesy

But I'm telling you it's true

It's really great to have a
dad

As wonderful as YOU!

a poem to say

You Are The Greatest

If someone was giving out medals

To say what a top dad you are
You would be told

You'd be getting the gold

Cos you are the greatest by far

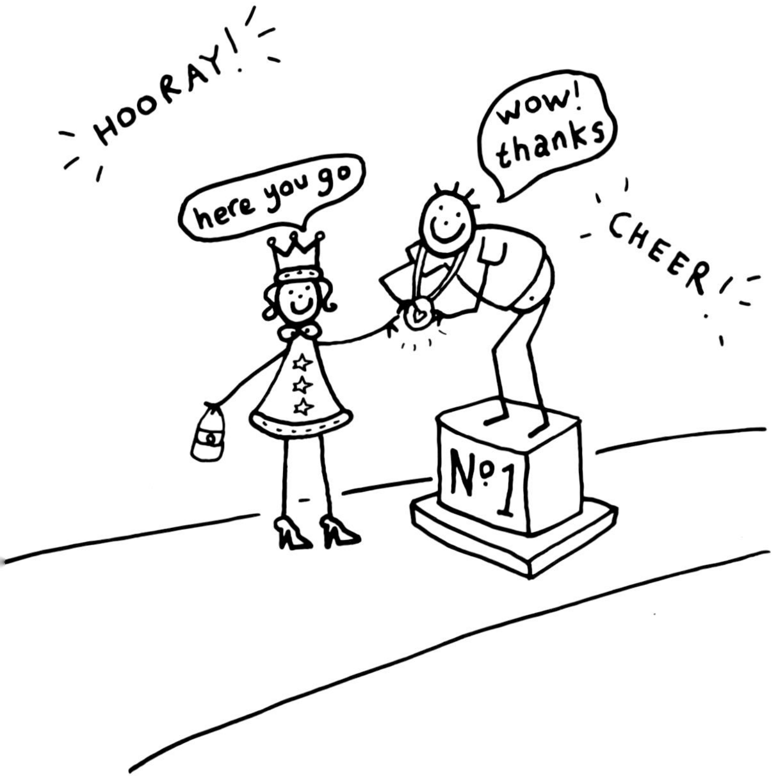
HOORAY!
here you go
wow! thanks
CHEER!
Nº1

Dads are sometimes
tempted to exaggerate
a little bit about their

a poem about

Getting Older

Your tummy's spreading out
a bit
Your hair is getting thinner
But none of that's important
Cos I say you're a winner!

a poem for

My Groovy Dad

Thanks for being so groovy

Thanks for being so mad

Thanks for being so totally
fab

Thanks for being my dad!

Some dads are stern and bossy, while some are really easy going.
It's just a matter of luck, really

a poem about my

Dad and Football

My Dad's a footie expert
He can hardly kick a ball,
But when it comes to
    armchair-playing

Woah! He knows it all!

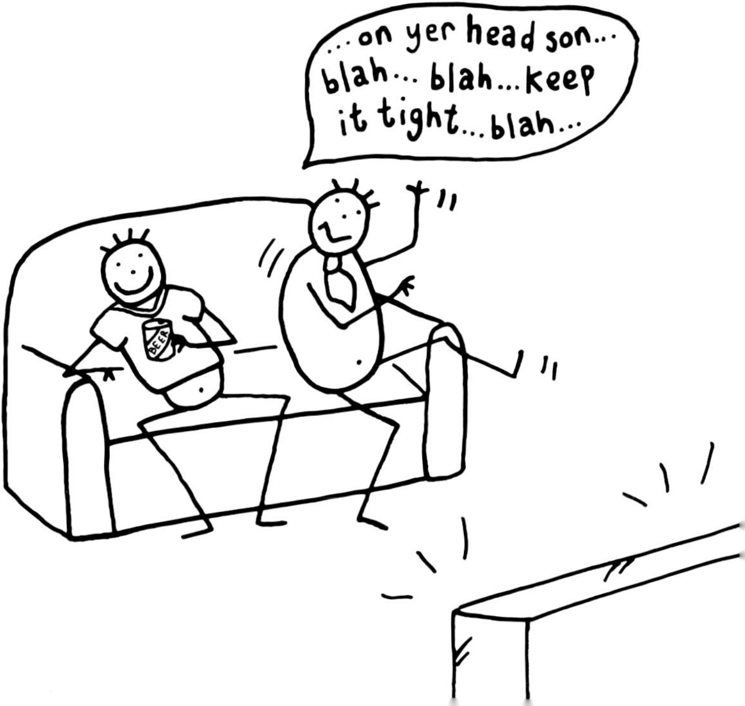
....on yer head son... blah... blah...keep it tight...blah...
BEER

a poem for my

Fabulous Dad

Some dads can be batty
And can drive you round
the bend
But you're not just a
brilliant one
You're also a fab friend!

Most dads know
a lot about something
or other

a poem about my dad

Being Right

My dad should be in
        Parliament

I've put him to the test

Whenever T.V. news comes on

He ALWAYS knows what's
        best

a poem about

Dads and Money

When the lawn needs mowing

Or the car could use a
wash

Tell your Dad you'll do it
for him...

If he'll dish the DOSH!

a poem for the

Best Dad Ever

Thanks for everything you
are
And all the things you do
There couldn't be another
dad
Who's half as great as YOU!

Thank you